ENDYMION

OR

The STATE *of* ENTROPY

Go thou to Rome—at once the Paradise,
The grave, the city, and the wilderness;
And where its wrecks like shatter'd mountains rise,
And flowering weeds, and fragrant copses dress
The bones of Desolation's nakedness
Pass, till the spirit of the spot shall lead
Thy footsteps to a slope of green access
Where, like an infant's smile, over the dead
A light of laughing flowers along the grass is spread;

—Percy Shelley, *Adonais.*

3

4

Ιερός Λόγος

ENDYMION

OR

The STATE
of ENTROPY

A LYRICAL DRAMA
INSCRIBED TO THE MEMORY OF
JOHN KEATS AND PERCY SHELLEY

❧

Kurt R. Ward
O.P.R.

Illustrations by Rebecca Yanovskaya
Design by Harry Huybers

AMSTERDAM
MMXXII.

CHORUS

The shades of Dawn begin to descend
As the Days subtle murmurs
Pass softly into Nights long dark train.
Day is but a shadow of the Senses,
A Cave which refracts all light,   5
Memories penumbral Chasm
Saturates each impending thought,
The eyes betray the Soul,
What our Silence cannot disguise.

Night is an infinite Prism,   10
A boundless plane of Spectral light,
Where Shadows weave a Masque of deception,
Unveiling what lie hidden by day,
In the Dark Stage of Night.

Now witness from out the East,   15
A storm rises over the Mortal plain,
The Winds converge to a flurried pace,
Their ranks' swell in formation,
Four by four downward sweep,
Darkening the veil of Heaven,   20
Shadowing Earth in tumult and rain.

Below, in the eye of the Tempest,
Where the Dusk from the West
Meets the Twilight of the East,   25
Urania weeps over the tombs of the Blessed,
Gone too soon...
For the Asphodel to crown their rest,
Endymion lies suspended in Dream
Above the grave of Adonais.   30

ACT I

A REVOLT *of* DISCORD

SCENE I.
The THRONE *of* OLYMPUS

Jupiter

The Forges of Tartarus smoulder
In the ashes of fallen Dreams,
The Titans cry out in Rebellion
As the Thresholds weaken.
Darkness obscure Empyrean!   5
Thunder Roar,
Lightning Quicken,
Storms Surge,
Tempest Blast,
Mountains Tremble,   10
Oceans Thrash,
Sever the bonds of Man's Sedition,
Withdraw Rites of Passage,
None dare siege the Light of Heaven,
Nor descend in Courage of Vision.   15

Diana

Thy torments are in vain,
You douse the Embers
Yet inflame Man's Desire.
All life strives to Ascend,
The infinite aspires in Nature,   20
The Sublime is distilled from the Profane.
The Pantheon of Olympus cannot subvert
The Reckoning of Hell and Heaven.

Jupiter

I rule in Absolutes,
My Reign is resolute,   25
Reason is Order,
Order transcends Truth.
The Emissaries of Saturn
Must not reclaim Sovereignty over intuition,
Man shall not kindle the Fire   30
The Titan has unjustly given.

Diana

The World and all you seek to possess
Withers from thy clutch
And with thee alone enslave.
Why suppress what cannot be restrained?   35
Logic cannot subvert Imagination,
The Laws of Science cannot Infinity divide,
Nor calculate Eternity in Divine proportion.

Jupiter

The Portals must be sealed,
Perception immersed in Cloud.   40
We must prevent the Immaterial below
Binding to the Incorruptible above,
Heaven must be indelible from Mundane,
Spirit subservient to Reason,
Nature bounded in Golden Chain.   45

ACT I

A REVOLT of DISCORD

SCENE II.
The THRONE of DIANA

Enter HERMES

Hermes

Jupiter and Saturn battle for position,
Mercury pivots between the Giants,
The Alignments stagger towards collision.
Typhon unleashes a venomous dye
That stains the starry Vestment,　　　　　　50
Earth's satellite swells the Ocean's Tides,
What Dark Force threatens
The balance of Creation?

Diana

Fierce Omens betray
What Shadows cannot hide,　　　　　　55
Saturn ascends as Jupiter declines.
In the face of withdrawal,
Jove commands the Winds to drive
Cloud and Storm over Rome's azure sky.
A Pall of Reason shrouds　　　　　　60
The Dreams of Endymion
To subvert Saturn's invincible rise.

Hermes

What banality should provoke
This warlike stance of Jove?
Prometheus pillared in rock,   65
The Titans usurped and dethroned.
Lapis altars turn to Bronze,
Emerald Tablets buried in stone.
The walls of Tartarus are inseparable
From the corruption of the Soul.   70
What power could force the might
Of Jupiter's unassailable Throne?

Diana

When the Conjunction reaches its Prime
The Pathways align at the Summit,
The Planets invert in the Transit,   75
Saturn accelerates in the formation,
Jupiter weakens out in the distance.
What the Monarch cannot conquer,
The Tyrant will seek to repress,
Therein lies Jupiter's vain obsession,   80
Light cannot penetrate the dark Descent,
What is revealed in Shadow,
Lies beyond the faculties of Cognition,
The Realm of Sleep has its own laws,
The Dreaming are immune   85
To the mechanics of Perception,
In the Twilight of unknowing,
The light of Reason dissolves.

Hermes

Man was meld from Earth
But conceived in the Heavens,   90
The way to Salvation lies
Through the duality of the Senses.
Deep within the Flame he stares,
Passion blind to Reason,
Reason blinded by Light,   95
The promontory of the Self
Is a double-barred Prison,
The closer to the truth,
The further it eludes his vision.

Diana

What is Beauty to the viper of Necessity   100
Coiled around the Mundane Shell?
The eyes glaze,
The Serpent strikes,
Each second becomes a day,
Each moment we Relapse.   105
The Path is forgotten,
The Keys are lost,
Only a God can navigate
The Labyrinths of Tartarus.

Hermes

The armies of Reason 110
Battle the Soul's dark Infantry,
Opposing and attracting with equal might,
The closer to the Zenith
The further repulsed,
Nearest the Cusp 115
The deeper they plummet,
One stray spark can divert their Orbit,
Courage must be ransomed with every Loss,
The same force that creates Life,
Can just as easily destroy it. 120

Diana

One moment of Joy exceeds
All the hours in Eternity,
The more you impose Order,
The greater the force of Entropy.
The Portals must be opened, 125
What is Above must also Descend,
The sanctity of Hell
Is the reprieve from Heaven,
If the two be not bound together,
The Dead cannot commune with the Living. 130

Hermes

We must tether the Winds
With a renewed purpose,
Release Winter into the arms of Spring,
Raise Paradise from the deluge.
Nature is not beholden unto Reason   135
Nor Chained to the logic of Order,
Zephyrus can temper the storms aggression,
Calm the burgeoning Tempest,
In the wake of Jupiter's oppression,
We shall lure Endymion   140
Into Shadow from out of Darkness.

Diana

Zephyrus cannot oppose the torrents of Jove
Nor stand against Winds of Misfortune,
Remorse inflicts a ceaseless toll,
Penitence will not grant Restitution.   145
What little Hope that still remains
Lies buried in a desert of Sin,
Unsealed but not forgotten,
Deep in the Isle of Souls.

Hermes

The scars of indifference 150
Map the deepest cuts,
Where the Arrows of Regret
Hold captive our Absolution.
No guilt will forgive
What the Heart cannot repent, 155
Confession betrays the Assassins,
In lamenting we exhume
What we Will to forget.

Diana

If the Maelstrom does not subside,
The Seals will be broken, 160
When the gates of Tartarus collapse,
The Devout become Forsaken.
Uncertainty devours on Faith,
Loneliness breeds Disconsolation,
Fear is the onset of retreat. 165
Each Bower shall be a Brier,
Each Blossom a Thorn.

Hermes

Doors without openings,
Windows without panes,
Worlds within worlds cross in-between,   170
Chapels in every meadow,
Sacristies in a winding brook,
Sanctuaries concealed under stone,
Cathedrals in the Wood,
Foundations of earth,   175
Heavens span the vault,
Amber laden columns,
Willows rising to an arch.

ACT II

The TREPIDATION *of* WIND

The CAVE *of* AEOLUS

Enter DIANA

Diana

Zephyrus speak to me of thy solemnity
With the diligence of Heart,
The World is weary from Inhibition,
Apathy wears the mask of Pride.
Why sequester from thy own volition   5
When Adversity should strengthen your resolve?
Rise with us in fearful opposition,
Bridle the Winds to our Sacred cause.

Zephyrus

The Way of Ascent is riddled
With the Litanies of the Dead,   10
Frozen Prophecies line
The charnels of the Mind,
Madness must be bartered
With each Epiphany won,
The Foundations cannot stand,   15
The reins may falter in the confusion,
None but a Fool is wise enough
To suffer Oblivion.

Diana

Those that force their way inside
Can never return the same,   20
For each dark and torpid Revelation,
The Dragons must be paid.
Nothing can be given
In the battle for Self Dominion,
Without the contrary gained.   25
Whosoever revokes the Way of Loss
Will find no release in Abandon,
The Candle must burn brighter
Than the Shadows it inflames.

Zephyrus

Scarce do we extinguish one Blaze   30
When another ignites within,
We must bind Reason to Sentiment,
Fortify the Citadel with great Trepidation.
What the Mind cannot retain,
No Logic can solve,   35
What the Heart cannot sustain,
No Grace may revive,
What the Spirit does not aspire to,
No Faith will imbibe,
In the State of Entropy,   40
The Face of Death is bitterly calm.

Diana

The Tyranny of Logic cannot absolve
The breaches that engulf Mind and Heart,
Smote the fire and the Spirit erupts,
The Soul is not deceived...   45
It knows intimately of Death.
Constancy within must be equal
To Disharmony without,
Winter must have its carnage
For the Spring to forgive the Frost.   50

Zephyrus

There is more death in Love's memory
Than in all the Gallows of Autumns rage,
A supreme fatality bestowed by Fate,
Which pierces too soon and slays too late.
Love cannot be deterred by Reason   55
Or saved from the logic of its own Demise,
What the Heart wills...
The Will cannot Divine.

Diana

Extremity is the road to Elation,
Adversity is bound with Delight,   60
Felicity and hardship flow together,
No Beauty without Tragedy,
No Concord without Strife,
We are unmapped inhabitants
Steering an uncharted course   65
Across the immensities of Desire and Loss,
Both must be circulated in equal measure,
Each granted at the dearest cost.

Zephyrus

Far lies the Soul,
Nearer lies the Heart,   70
The Iniquity cannot be crossed,
No hope will raise a ladder enough
To scale the Tower of Solace,
Longing cannot surmount the distance
Between desire and despair.   75

Diana

The greater the Suffering,
The more inexpressible the Lament,
What you repress in Sublimation
Permeates until manifest.
Fear is the Sacrament,   80
Pain the Host,
The deeper the Harrowing
The greater the Ascent,
The only way out of Sorrow
Is to surrender to Loss.   85

Zephyrus

Does the Wolf pursue from hunger
Or flee from Lust?
To love one must possess,
Passion seeks only an end unto itself,
The hunter is the hunted,   90
Our prey becomes the Devout,
The Quarry we seek is only ourselves.

Diana

Where is the promise that awakens
From the union of Day and Night?
The Fruits of Despair 95
Rot on the shores of the Unwept,
Let us name the un-nameable,
Fear named is destroyed,
There is power in Forgiveness,
Harmony in a trembling Voice. 100

Zephyrus

If to love is to live,
Why does Death hide behind each kiss?
Pity not the Dead but the dying,
Who must endure the irredeemable Curse.
Let me linger in my Silence, 105
The Unspoken need not grieve,
There is not enough compassion
To heal the wounds inflicted in Suffering.

Diana

Pain has no precedence,
Affliction is a singular Pact, 110
A splinter on the Soul,
A noose around the Past.
One can do naught but suffer,
Anguish must come out
In reparation or in recompense. 115

Zephyrus

I once loved,
I knew not else,
From all worldly things blind,
That consummating Joy,
The pain of divided Self,   120
The artifice of Ideal,
Clarity of Purpose,
Until the last whisper of Hope
Dissolved in fields of Mourning,
Where Love lies quivering   125
In the cold and frost.

Diana

What you Fear is not what is lost,
But what you have not Found,
The Mirror conceals more
Than what the Lamp can reveal.   130
There is not a sighing in the wind
That hope cannot amend,
Love exceeds our Monarchial pain,
What Discord divides,
Nature will restore,   135
Pain is transient,
The Spirit endures.
Unearth thy true Emanation,
Release the Deity within.

ACT III

The RITES *of* PASSAGE

ENGLISH CEMETERY *in* ROME

Enter HERMES

Endymion

As if Mind were sky,
Body the ground,
I am vanquished in Shadow,
Decay hangs motionless in Ruins,
Ramparts cower beneath the strain,   5
All cohesion gone.
What shades this dim Dream?
How do I differentiate from
What is and what merely seems?

Hermes

How thin the veil   10
Between Thought and Dream,
How narrow the chasm of Day and Night,
Where do they meet,
Where do they converge?
To which do we awaken,   15
From which emerge?
What ineffable Sinew binds between?
What initiates in Dream
Is consummated in Light,
In rising we Fall,   20
In falling we Ascend.

Endymion

Far from the shore of Man
I am adrift in torments of Doubt,
There is rancour in the Wind,
The scent of Sulphur on the marsh.   25
What invisible hand drapes their Shadow
On this pale and shallow plot?
What are the Idylls of Imagination
To the dark Sentinels that besiege
The Fortress of my Thoughts?   30

Hermes

We are the reflections in the Mirror
The moment you look aside,
The Faces in the clouds,
The Whispers echoed from afar,
The grin on your Lover's face   35
When the parting is through,
The Lies that conceal the truth,
The Truth that lies to reveal,
We are the Past you failed to grieve
When the grieving is past,   40
We are the Inner way beneath the Outer path,
The architect of Basilica and Obelisk.

Endymion

Why should my heart
Vexed with the insurrection of Birth
Be more silent than this Grave?   45
Dawn spurns my every advance,
The trees reach out for my hand
With each branch but I don't feel it.
The Past is calling out my name
Like some soft-spoken dream,   50
A half-remembered refrain,
A vague familiar glance,
But I don't hear it.
From whence do we come?
The further we move ahead,   55
The more we stumble behind.

Hermes

Like Orphans we look into
The arms of Night,
Drowning in the uncertainty
Of our own Reflection.   60
Between Dog and Wolf
We are born unbidden,
Shadows from out the distant flame.
Looking forward we look back again,
Sedentary slumbers and Lethargic rites,   65
Memories gleam past like receding tides,
What is unwritten is unseen,
The Future an illusion,
Neither what is nor what should be.

Endymion

I stand upon a solitary Shore   70
Thirsting with insatiable drought,
For one sign of Redemption
To quiet this obstinate doubt,
To know that Birth and Life are more
Than the sum of our conceited Arts,   75
To reconcile the Impermanence of all things
Against our everlasting Desire.
We are rooted in Reverie,
Confined in conceits of Pride,
The hypocrisy of knowledge   80
Is the futility for the Divine,
Perhaps only in Death,
Is there meaning in Life.

Hermes

Hold Time against the chasm of Space,
Is it nonetheless permanent?   85
Look into thy Imperial Hand,
Does it not also contain the Infinite?
Are we not born from out that same Flame?
Though each must serve their own Fate,
Cannot both serve a higher Purpose?   90

Endymion

The Precipice is too steep,
Darkness bounds in each direction,
There is barely a thread to cling,
Sheltered in Desolation,
Gasping for a semblance of Being,   95
The tacit mirrors of Recrimination
Fracture from without,
Obscure from within.

Hermes

Not alone what you seek you will find,
Not all you find may never have been lost.   100
The Path is solitary and dangerous,
The Expanse is narrow and deep,
Knowledge frees but soon enslaves.
Be wary of double meanings,
Be mindful of weary thoughts,   105
Wisdom comes not from the Mind
But is endowed by Heart,
In Unknowing there is Knowing,
To know the Infinite without,
Seek the Finite within.   110

Endymion

Which Path do I choose
With no clarity of direction?
How do I scale irreconcilable Heights
When grounded with Indecision?
How do you navigate in Shadow   115
Under the cloud of Perception?
I regress when I should recoil
From the Minds dark deceptions.

Hermes

The Summoned will be called,
Unanswered consigned,   120
Once you open the doors on God,
The Labyrinth must be crossed.
Behind you lies the endless Horizon,
Ahead a towering Abyss,
Above a beckoning Silence   125
Below a Heaven of Dissonance.

ACT IV

The PERPETUAL PYRE

SCENE I.
CHTHONIAN CAVE

Enter ENDYMION

Diana —— Hekate

With Ancient words I entreat
The winding sheet of Memory,
Unveil the Spirits cloaked in dream,
Invoke the Daemons that awake our Sleep,
Summon the daughters of Mnemosyne   5
To consummate the Auguries of Discontent.

In Dream,
I dreamt I could not wake,
Sleep swept along my living veins
Like an anchor to my Mortal frame.   10
My body sank in silence,
One by one Sorrows came,
Solitude led the way,
She laid herself full down
Above my head where the grass grew long.   15
Innocence followed frail and afraid,
She closed my eyes and folded my arms.
Melancholy came dour and grave,
Spread Myrrh and Frankincense over the fray.
Love came last to join the throng,   20
Weak and fragile where she lay,
She said a Prayer of mournful song,
Then set the Liturgy ablaze.

The Spirit bears the mortar of Indifference,
Memory is the ground on which it is laid.   25
What is past now has no presence,
The future reframed.
A Copse in the Dusk has broken,
Nothing that is awoken,
Shall slumber again.   30

ACT IV

The PERPETUAL PYRE

SCENE II.
DARK FOREST GROVE

Enter ENDYMION

Diana——Artemis

With Ancient words I entreat
The winding sheet of Memory,
Unfold the Tapestry of Fate,
Summon Ambassadors
From Earth, Forest and Ocean,   35
Unfurl the provenance of the Past,
To the providence of the Living.

In Dream I descend,
The Double Helix unwinds,
Now a single solitary Strand   40
Rises amid Volcanic Spires,
Carbon filaments unite Sulfur and Iron
Until a Spark ignites from out the Mire,
Swelling the Oceans,
Surging across the Land.   45
Down the millennia I pass,
The Stairway extends,
From River to Forest,
To Air and grassy Plain,
Predator, Disease, Drought and Plague   50
Lash and assail at each advancing stage,
Yet the Ribbon ever expands,
Now exposing the Signature of Man.
Death's long Shadows fly,
From Mother to Daughter,   55
From Daughter to Son,
Famine, Poverty, Avarice and Guile
Impede but cannot suspend,
The immutable Ascent
From which all Life stems.   60

Who weeps for Birds that do not sing,
Or the Amaranth too sensitive to outlast?
There is no record of what might have been,
Nor of what that did not come to pass.
When one thread is cut,   65
Two more are frayed,
The Web of Being is spun,
Fate cannot still the unremitting Path,
Eternity rests for none.
Past is now unwritten,   70
Future is now past.

ACT IV

The PERPETUAL PYRE

SCENE III.
L U N A

Enter E N D Y M I O N

Diana —— Selene

With Ancient words I entreat
The winding sheet of Memory,
Summon Demiurge from out Creation,
Withdraw Form and Shape,   75
Forge Chaos from Oblivion,
Divide Nucleus from Atom.

Endymion

I dreamt a Dream,
A dream divine,
World without Shadow,   80
Darkness consumes the horizon,
Nothing stirs in the Hollow,
The Universe a barren womb.
Thrice I trace a Spiral round,
Then encircle them in Proportion,   85
With Golden Mean I multiply them,
Igniting Forges of Dawn.
Helium and Hydrogen combine,
Atoms gather Protons,
Neutrons birth Stars,   90
Planets orbit and Galaxies collide,
Suns are reborn, recede and die.
The Light shines out through me
Reflecting back unto Eternity.

When you look in the eyes of the Precipice,   95
The Soul in silence resounds,
The Veil that hides the Infinite...
Tatters in the Reflection,
Matter and Spirit coalesce,
Universe weds Dark to Light,   100
First bound to Last,
Infinities enclosed into One.

ACT IV

The PERPETUAL PYRE

Enter DIANA

Endymion

Weightless I bear the Immense
Unwinding of the Infinite,
Against our bare Inconsequence.   105
Waves of Consolation flood my senses,
Rapture emanates to Delight,
Tabernacles of Sorrow crown my vision,
Anguish and Elation tower and plummet,
Shattered with Sensation,   110
Breathless in Twilight.

Diana

When the Thresholds of experience
Exceed the boundaries of Perception,
The Pathways overflow,
We are battered by Empathy, 115
Bewildered in the outpouring of Soul.
The Spirit yields to brief destruction,
The Triumph of Joy,
In the abundance of Awe.

Endymion

Star upon Star, 120
Soul over Soul
Wash over me in Sorrow,
The Venerated and Forlorn,
The Solemn and Downcast,
Swept in their unwavering path, 125
The River ever runs down,
Down to the depths of Despairing,
Down to the bedlam of Regret.

Diana

Lost in the disparity of Shadows,
The Soul in absentia yearns to unite,   130
Darkness must Eclipse,
We grasp at Stars but gather only Dust,
Night looms constant on the Horizon,
Yet the Heavens bring no respite,
In the disunity of Spirit and Mind.   135

Endymion

How do I take forward
What was brought back,
Retrieve what is no longer Bereft,
Articulate what can be only Sensed?
Every word yields more Questions,   140
Each line is embellished with Doubt.
What is Authentic and what is Delusion?
How do I translate Allegory from Allusion,
Without the certainty of Truth?

Diana

Extract only Essence,   145
Evoke what has been diffused,
The Unconscious must be boldly transcribed,
The Art of Memory is subterfuge,
Each must their own Conscience abide.
What was Concealed must be deciphered,   150
Uncover what has been Subdued,
What we reveal in Symbol,
Is beyond what Language can divulge,
What lies dormant in prose,
Poetry can distill,   155
What Poetry cannot instill,
Only music can bestow.

Endymion

The Dew falls and soon gone again,
Only Fragments now remain,
I am diminished with Apprehension,   160
Lost in the aftermath of dismay.
Have I persevered over Shadow,
Only to succumb to Dissolution?
Am I the Actor or Author,
Of this unwritten play?   165

Diana

Life suspends from impenetrable Opposition,
The Paths must be forged again and again,
Nothing remains in isolation,
Constellations transit,
Alignments wane,   170
Stars collapse and fuse in Fire,
Expanding and contracting,
Forging new worlds in their flames.
Worlds begin where the Universe ends,
As each are an ember,   175
Of the Perpetual Pyre.

CHORUS

Some are born into Darkness,
Some born from out of Light,
The Firmament of Man
Extends from Within to Without.
Soul and Spirit are equidistant   5
As Mind from Thought.
We teeter in the balance,
Struggling to defy the plot,
The Poet must become a Prophet,
The Fool transform to a Sage,   10
The King master Philosophy,
The Priest freed from Faith.
The Denizens of Light conspire
To gain the knowledge of Perdition,
While Titans desire the rapture of Heaven.   15
What we consecrate by Night,
Must be affirmed in the vigilance of Day.

FINIS.

 the image contains the text "ASMENOS EK THANATOIO" on a pyramid.

"The Greek tragic writers, in selecting as their
subject any portion of their national history or
mythology, employed in their treatment of it a
certain arbitrary discretion. They by no means
conceived themselves bound to adhere to the
common interpretation or to imitate in story
as in title their rivals and predecessors."

—Percy Shelley, *Prometheus Unbound.*

ARCHAIC SYMBOLS,
LITERARY REFERENCES,
EDITORIAL COMMENTARIES
AND COINCIDENCES

Most of the inner
dialogues of this poem
transpired between the ages of
twenty-three and twenty-seven.

The following notes and references
were invaluable in piecing together
the fragments of that experience
and in deciphering the symbols
for this publication.

TITLE PAGES AND CHORUS

P. 4 The Protestant Cemetery in Rome is also known as the
Englishmen's Cemetery or the Cemetery of Artists and Poets
and is located in the area of Testaccio. Both JOHN KEATS and
PERCY SHELLEY have graves here.

P. 4 The Pyramid of Cestius, which is now situated inside the
cemetery walls, was built from between 18 and 12 BC as
a tomb for a Priest of Jupiter. Ancient manuscripts mention
a pyramid called Abou Hermes that was built in Memphis that
supposedly contained Hermes tomb and writings.

P. 5 The Greek text Ιερός Λόγος is taken from *the Orphic fragments*
collected by OTTO KERN, of which some are dated at the
beginning of the third century BC. Loosely translated as
'Sacred Logos'.

P. 5 Endymion is derived from the Ancient Greek name "Endumíon"
(Ἐνδυμίων), from "Endyein (ενδυειν)" which means 'to
dive into, to enter'. CLAUDE DE WARREN in *Interpretation des
Mythes Greces* describes him as "the one whose conscience is
consecrated."

P. 5 John Keats died from tuberculosis on February 23, 1821 in
Rome, Italy. Percy Shelley died by drowning on July 8, 1822 in
the Gulf of Sperzia, Italy. Keats dedicated *Endymion* to the poet
Thomas Chatterton.

L. 8 The ancient Egyptians held that the eyes are the seat of the
soul, "Osiris is hidden in the eye of Horus."

L. 9 "For we wrestle not against flesh and blood, but against
principalities, against powers, against the rulers of the darkness
of this world, against spiritual wickedness in high places." *King
James Bible, Ephesians* 6:12.

L. 13 "The psychic is a phenomenal world in itself, which can be reduced neither to the brain nor to metaphysics." "Long before they reach consciousness, certain unconscious tendencies betray their presence by symbols, occurring mostly in dreams but also in waking fantasies and symbolic action." CARL JUNG, *Mysterium Coniunctionis*.

L. 17 Aeolus was the divine keeper of the winds and king of the floating island of Aeolia. He kept the violent winds locked safely away inside the cavernous interior of his isle, releasing them only at the command of the greatest gods to wreak devastation upon the world.

L. 26 Urania is a Greek Muse who represents astronomy, the constellations and philosophy. She was the daughter of Zeus and Mnemosyne. Her name derives from the Greek word for 'heavenly'. JOHN MILTON invokes her in *Paradise Lost* as does PERCY SHELLEY in *Adonais*.

L. 28 "Hermes, the Helper, led them down the dank ways. Past the streams of Oceanus they went, past the rock Leucas, past the gates of the sun and the land of dreams, and quickly came to the mead of asphodel, where the spirits dwell, phantoms of men who have done with toils." Homer, *Odyssey*.

L. 30 PERCY SHELLEY's *Adonias* is an elegy on the death of John Keats. Shelley could be alluding to the myth of Adonis, the handsome young Greek who was equally admired by Aphrodite by Persephone. When they were unable to agree on which Goddess shall have him, Zeus decided Adonis would spend half the year on Earth with Aphrodite and half the year in the underworld with Persephone. Adonai is a Hebrew word, which means Lord and is a term used of both God and humans.

ACT I — A REVOLT OF DISCORD

L. 1   Tartarus are the infernal regions of ancient Greek mythology.
It is also a personification of a worldly element, who along
with Gaea [Earth] produced the daemon Typhon who tried to
overthrow the Olympians. In ancient Orphic texts it is also the
unbounded first existing entity from which the Light and the
Cosmos are born.

L. 3   The Olympians are the gods who ruled after Zeus led his siblings
to overthrow Saturn and the Titans. They lived on Mount
Olympus which was regarded as the abode of the gods and the
site of his throne.

L. 5   Jupiter is called the God of the Dark Sky and controlled the
weather and was often described as 'the gatherer of clouds'.
He watches over justice and truth, and is therefore also the
god of oaths and who must show his approval or disapproval
of contemplative undertakings.

L. 9   "Let not Zeus be angry again." "and pour down showers
of rain through the air to flood the circuit of the eternal
universe. I hope I may not behold the sea in the sky and
Selene's car soaking." NONNUS OF PANOPOLIS, *The Dionysiaca.*

L. 15   "He ne'er is crown'd With immortality, who fears to follow
Where airy voices lead: so through the hollow, The silent
mysteries of earth, descend!" JOHN KEATS, *Endymion.*

L. 16   Diana's name is derived from the Latin word dius which
means 'godly' and divios which means 'divine, heavenly'.
She was a virgin goddess who roamed the wilderness as the
goddess of the hunt, the goddess of the moon and often
described as 'she who hunts the clouds

L. 25 After the revolt of the Titans, Zeus and his brothers divided the universe into three realms. Poseidon became king of the oceans and seas, Hades the ruler of the Underworld and Zeus was given domain over the sky and the air and recognized as ruler of the Olympians.

L. 31 Prometheus created man from a lump of clay in the image of the gods and allowed him to walk upright so that he might look towards the heavens. However, when Prometheus saw that life was difficult for man, he defied the will of Zeus and stole fire from the gods and taught man how to craft tools and instructed him how to live through agriculture.

L. 37 Isaac Newton is most commonly known for his scientific discoveries but also produced many works on occult studies.

L. 41 "According to the ancients, lovelier than reason is sacred madness." PLATO, *Phaedrus*.

L. 45 "Hang me a golden chain from heaven, and lay hold of it all of you, gods and goddesses together - tug as you will, you will not drag Zeus the supreme counselor from heaven to earth." HOMER, *Iliad*.

L. 46 BOCCACCIO'S *On the Genealogy of the Gods of the Gentiles* describes Hermes as the "interpreter of secrets and the dissolver of the clouds of the mind" and "it is Mercury's part to control the winds". In other mythology texts he is called the 'companion of black night'. The Greeks related the Egyptian god Thoth to Hermes due to his similar attributes and functions and later became known as The Thrice Great Hermes Trismegistus. Hermes is also described as the deity which presides over rational energy, unfolds into light intellectual gifts, fills all things with divine reasons, elevates souls to intellect and wakens them from profound sleep.

L. 56 Saturn was the King of the Titans and his mythological reign was depicted as a Golden Age of plenty and peace. As Cronus, he represented time, in particular time as a destructive, all-devouring force. Saturn fathered Jupiter, Neptune, Pluto, Juno, Ceres and Vesta.

L. 60 "This is the wall of paradise, and it is there in paradise that you reside. The wall's gate is guarded by the highest spirit of reason, and unless it is overpowered, the way in will not lie open." NICHOLAS CUSA, *De Visione Dei.*

L. 61 At Endymion's request, Zeus granted him eternal sleep. CLAUDE DE WARREN regards this as: "a symbol of the disappearance of the ego. This allows the true personality represented by Selene, daughter of Hyperion, to take its rightful place in the evolution of the adventurer."

L. 62 Saturn is often called the dark malefic star. In Cabbalism, Saturn is the third sphere of divine activity, understanding or intelligence. This is the power which organizes the creative forces and imposes form on the universe.

L. 65 Prometheus was depicted in *Prometheus Bound* by AESCHYLUS as the bringer of fire and civilization to mortals as well giving man all the arts and sciences and the means of survival. In revenge for giving man fire, Zeus had him nailed to a mountain in the Caucasus and sent an eagle each day to eat his regenerating liver.

L. 66 Cronus [Saturn] married his sister Rhea, but it was prophesied that one of his own sons would dethrone him. He ate all his children but when he tried to swallow Zeus, Rhea tricked him and he ate a stone instead. Zeus later used a potion to make Zeus vomit up his brothers and sisters. They sprang out unhurt and in gratitude asked him to lead them in a war against his father and the other Titans. The war lasted 10 years until Zeus released the Cyclops and Hundred-handed Ones from Tartarus to help in the fight. While Hades and Poseidon distracted Cronus, Zeus struck him down with a thunderbolt. The Titans were finally defeated and were banished to Tartarus while Saturn was said to be exiled to Italy.

L. 73 In cosmology, a triple conjunction occurs when three planets align in the night sky as seen from Earth. Jupiter, Saturn, and Mercury each take a very different amount of time to orbit the sun. Saturn takes 29 years, Jupiter 12 years, and Mercury 88 days.

L. 81 PAUSANIAS in his *Description of Greece* gives an unusual version of how Orpheus the poet died after he went down to Hades to ask for his wife Eurydice to be returned to the living. "Some say that Orpheus came to his end by being struck by a thunderbolt, hurled at him by the god [Zeus] because he revealed sayings in the mysteries to men who had not heard them before."

L. 95 "The stirrings in the darkness necessarily seem like a devilish betrayal of the ideal of spiritual development. Reason cannot help in spite of all evidence to the contrary. Morality can permit itself no capacity for change, for whatever it does not agree with is inevitably immoral and has therefore to be repressed." CARL JUNG, *Aspects of the Masculine.*

L. 111 "Just as there are three main powers in fire—heat, light, and fleeting subtlety—so there are three similar powers in the soul's essence: the power of life, of understanding, and of desiring.... At different times the soul brings forth its variety of seeds more or less in profusion." MARSILIO FICINO, *Commentary on Plato's Phaedrus.*

L. 116 In Cosmology, Jupiter's constant gravitational pulling could over a long period of time accumulate and pull Mercury off course so immensely that it could eject the planet from the Solar System or send it on a collision course with other celestial bodies.

L. 119 There is a theory that during the formation of the planets, Jupiter's orbit moved drastically towards the sun which may have prevented additional gas giants forming. The gravity was so great that it pulled in ice meteors from the outer system towards earth which could explain the abundance of water on earth. Saturn's gravity eventually pulled Jupiter back out again away from the sun and the Earth, which could have collided has they continued.

L. 125 There are records in Rome's ancient history of a Mundus of Ceres, an underground vault that was sealed by a stone lid called the lapis manalis. It is said that the opening separated the living world from the underworld and offered the spirits of the dead temporary leave from the underworld to roam among the living.

L. 130 The Greek word Daimon means 'provider or divider of fortunes or destinies'.

L. 131　The Anemoi are the Winds who originate from the four corners. Each has a specific task and are often summoned to intervene in human endeavours. The Anemoi can support or obstruct but are usually characterized as objective forces. Curiously, Poseidon, who reigns the subconscious, is often shown as the master of the winds in many Greek epics. The Roman poet STATIUS in *Thebaid* claims Zeus has the power to loosen "the reins of winds and tempests, and sends alternate hurricanes to afflict the world, opposing forces meet in heaven."

L. 132　CLAUDE DE WARREN says that HESIOD in *Theogony* declares that "the winds were born from The Dawn and the Stars" and thus they are "awakenings of consciousness" "to help the return journey towards Unity." He also describes Zephyrus as "a symbol of divine aid for Achilles to free himself of all traces of the grip of these past realisations" "It is therefore a purification which the seeker cannot carry out through his own forces alone."

L. 140　"Hermes governs the different herds of souls, and disperses the sleep and oblivion with which they are oppressed. He is likewise the supplier of recollection, the end of which is a genuine intellectual apprehension of divine natures." PROCLUS, *Comment on First Alcibiades.*

L. 142　Zephyrus is the West Wind. HOMER describes him as "unleashing the violence of autumn storms which causes the fall of dead leaves and branches." But according to HESIOD, he "lightens the sky." His name is referenced as meaning 'watering down from the top to the bottom' and is therefore also seen as a force of purification by cleansing the past.

L. 146　Zeus in revenge for Prometheus giving fire to man punished humanity and instructed Hephaestus to fashion a maiden out of earth, clay and water. The gods showered her with gifts. She was called Pandora which means 'all gift' and given to Prometheus's brother, the Titan Epimetheus. Such was her beauty that he took Pandora as his wife.

On their wedding day Zeus presented her with a beautiful box on the condition that she must never open it. Because Pandora had also been endowed with curiosity, she opened the box and released disease, famine, poverty, misery and sadness. Only hope remained in the box before she was able to seal it again.

L. 161　Liminal deities preside over thresholds, gates, or doorways and can cross boundaries of the underworld. Both Hermes and Diana [Hekate] were guardians of the netherworld and had roles to transport souls. They act as guardians of all journeys including the journey to the afterlife. Hekate is often shown with Hermes in guiding Persephone back from the underworld with torches.

ACT II — THE TREPIDATION OF WIND

L. 10   "One is harassed, both day and night, by the divine being that is the image of the living self within the locked labyrinth of one's own disoriented psyche." JOSEPH CAMPBELL, *The Hero with a Thousand Faces*.

L. 19   "If the demand for self knowledge is willed by fate and is refused, this negative attitude may end in real death" "the subliminal contents already possess such a high energy charge that, when afforded an outlet by active imagination, they may overpower the conscious mind and take possession of the personality." CARL JUNG, *Mysterium Coniunctionis*.

L. 26   "Whoever goes uninitiated and unsanctified to the other world will lie in the mire, but he who arrives there initiated and purified will dwell with the gods." PLATO, *Phaedo*.

L. 31   "The gods have become diseases; Zeus no longer rules Olympus but rather the solar plexus, and produces curious specimens for the doctor's consulting room, or disorders the brains of politicians and journalists who unwittingly let loose psychic epidemics on the world." CARL JUNG, *Alchemical Studies*.

L. 74   "The union of opposites on a higher level of consciousness is not a rational thing, nor is it a matter of will; it is a process of psychic development that expresses itself in symbols." CARL JUNG, *Commentary on the Secret of the Golden Flower*.

L. 82   Hermes "is that consciousness which keeps the experience of life and death inseparable. As the God of thresholds Hermes is open to both life and death equally and sees no opposition between them." NOEL COBB, *Archetypal Imagination*.

L. 82   The Harrowing of Hell is the triumphant descent of Christ into Hell as described in the *King James Bible, Peter* 1. *The Epic of Gilgamesh* and HOMER's *Odyssey* also include a descent. VIRGIL's *Aeneid* includes a reference to the Eleusinian Mysteries rituals of the death and rebirth of the initiate.

L. 94   Equinox comes from the Latin word aequus, meaning 'equal', and nox, meaning 'night'. This is the day that night-time and day-time are approximately 12 hours each all over the world.

L. 114   "Always it comes about that the beginning of wisdom is a fear." MIGUEL DE UNNAMUMO, *The Tragic Sense of Life*.

L. 116   Zephyrus competed with the god Apollo for the love of Hyacinthus, a young and handsome prince. Apollo became the lover of the young man, making Zephyrus crazy with jealousy. One day when they were practicing discus throwing, Zephyrus blew a strong gust of wind which diverted the discus from its course and killed Hyacinthus. Apollo created the flower that bears his name.

L. 124   In VIRGIL's *Aeneid*, the Mourning Fields was a space in the underworld reserved for souls who wasted their lives on unrequited love.

L. 129   "The symbol reveals certain aspects of reality - the deepest aspects - which defy any other means of knowledge. Images, symbols and myths are not irresponsible creations of the psyche; they respond to a need and fulfil a function, that of bringing to light the most hidden modalities of being." MIRCEA ELIADE, *Images and Symbols*.

ACT III — THE RITES OF PASSAGE

L. 6   "One does not discover new lands without consenting to lose sight of the shore for a very long time." Andre Gide, *The Counterfeiters*.

L. 10   According to HYGINUS in *Astronomica*, Perseus received from Hermes "a helmet which kept its wearer from being seen" "the helmet of Hades [the Unseen One]." Hermes is often described as the Ruler of Dream. "Now Cyllenian Hermes called away the suitors' ghosts, holding firm in his hand the wand of fine pure gold that enchanted the eyes of men whenever Hermes wants or wakes us up from sleep." HOMER, *The Odyssey*.

L. 31   "Let us then imagine archetypes as the deepest patterns of psychic functioning, the roots of the soul governing the perspectives we have of ourselves and the world. They are the axiomatic, self-evident images to which psychic life and our theories about it ever return." JAMES HILLMAN, *Re-Visioning Psychology*.

L. 37   "We are arrant knaves, all; believe none of us." William SHAKESPEARE, *Hamlet*.

L. 41   KARL KERENYI in *Hermes* says that he escorts and protects heroes in perilous enterprises, and gives them prudent counsels as "the one who leads souls away and leads them back again."

L. 80   "Since no knowledge is better than that by which man knows himself, let us examine our thoughts, words, and deeds. For what does it avail us if we are to investigate carefully and understand rightly the nature of all things, yet do not understand ourselves?" ANONYMOUS, *Liber de Spiritu et Anima*.

L. 88   "This world order, the same for all, no god made or any man, but it always was and is and will be an ever-living fire, kindling by measure and going out by measure." HERACLITUS, *Fragments*.

L. 101 "These encroachments upon the darkness are not without danger. Dreaming has it's own dead, the insane." "The dreamer must be stronger than the dream." VICTOR HUGO, *William Shakespeare.*

L. 110 "Do not go outside, return to within yourself; truth dwells in the inner man; and if you find that your nature is changeable, transcend yourself." AUGUSTINUS VAN HIPPO, *Of True Religion.*

L. 111 "Thou canst not travel on the Path before thou hast become that Path itself." HELENA PETROVNA BLAVATSKY, *The Voice of the Silence.*

L. 114 "I see that you believe these things are true because I say them. Yet, you do not see how. Thus, though believed, their truth is hidden from you." DANTE ALIGHERI, *The Paradiso.*

L. 119 "If you believe you are the master of your soul become its servant. If you are her servant become her master." CARL JUNG, *Liber Novus.*

L. 121 "God is not a Mind, but the Cause that the Mind is; not a Spirit, but the Cause that the Spirit is; not Light, but the Cause that Light is." *The Divine Pymander of Hermes Mercurius Trismegistus.*

ACT IV — THE PERPETUAL PYRE

P. 43   Greek religious poetry which dealt with death and the world beyond the grave refer to deities whose influence was exercised in the underworld. These deities are a separate class from the Olympians and were called the Chthonian gods.

P. 43   "Below that haunted cave of fair-haired Nymphs Where, as Endymion slept beside his kine, Divine Selene watched him from on high, And slid from heaven to earth; for passionate love Drew down the immortal stainless Queen of Night." SMYRNAEUS QUINTUS, *The Fall of Troy*.

L. 1   SENECA in *Medea* evokes the triple goddess of Diana, Selene, and Hekate. She symbolizes the crossroads which are the paths lit by the full moon to make choices 'in the dark' without the light of guidance. *The Chaldean Oracles* represent Hekate as the function of the World Soul which combines with ideas to perfect the sensible world.

L. 3   Hekate is a protector against evil spirits and is worshipped as a guide to help others transition to the "other side". THEOCRITUS describes her as "holder of the keys that can unlock the gates between realms and unlock the gates of death." VIRGIL describes the entrance to hell as 'Hekate's Grove'. Hekate mediated between Olympians and Titans as well as mortals and divine spheres. HESIOD says that Zeus made her "a nurse of the young who after that day saw with their eyes the light of all-seeing Dawn".

L. 4   Book IX of HOMERS *Odyssey* is called Nekuia, which is an ancient Greek rite used to summon and question ghosts.

L. 5   Mnemosyne was the goddess of memory and remembrance and the inventor of language and words. She was the mother of the nine Muses that inspired artists, poets and philosophers in creativity.

L. 31 Claude de Warren interprets Artemis: "She represents the feminine aspect of the force of light and truth that leads man towards the contact and union with the psychic, and which will then open the door to the world of spirit and allow the descent of the latter into the inferior planes, preparing the process of transformation. Artemis is the force responsible for making integrity grow. She is the 'will of the soul' or 'the illuminated will'."

L. 33 The Moirai are known better as the Fates who controlled the mother thread of life of every mortal from birth to death. They were independent and guarded that the fate assigned to every being shall take its course without obstruction. Curiously there are cryptic references to the Orphics having associated the Fates with the three divisions of Selene: the crescent moon, full moon, and dark moon.

L. 42 All life on earth was comprised from carbon, nitrogen, oxygen, sulphur and phosphorus.

L. 46 HESIOD describes a mythological five ages of man in *Works and Days*. The Golden Age was the reign of Saturn [Cronus] in which a golden race of humanity lived without cares but are all gone. The last age of man is described as the Iron Age, when men live in toil and misery. Because they are degenerate, cruel, unjust, malicious, and treacherous, the gods have forsaken humanity.

L. 62 The Amaranth is a never fading flower which symbolizes immortality.

L. 72 Claude de Warren's interpretation of Selene: "She is the symbol of a light reflected on the planes of the spirit, a greater self and a receptive and executive state of consciousness" "she is the symbol of the incarnated self of supramental man, a symbol of complete dedication and of a perfect giving of oneself."

L. 74 In PLATO's *Timaeus*, the Demiurge was the creator of the universe and imposed order on chaos. The Gnostics used it as term for deities who ruled the material world.

L. 88 Hydrogen and helium account for nearly all the nuclear matter in today's universe. This is consistent with the big bang model.

L. 89 It took about 380,000 years for electrons to be trapped in orbits around nuclei, forming the first atoms.

L. 103 "The confrontation of conscious [rational] data with those that are unconscious [irrational] necessarily results in a modification of standpoint." CARL JUNG, *Mysterium Coniunctionis.*

L. 112 This perceptible inadequacy of the earthily bodily form as the expression and instrument of the spirit dwelling within is the undefined, driving thought which becomes the basis of all true thoughts — the cause of the evolution of intelligence — that which obliges us to assume an intelligible world and an infinite series of expressions and instruments of each spirit, whose index or root is its individuality." NOVALIS, *The Athenaeum Journal, Easter* 1798.

L. 116 "Genuine imagination is inspired by the unconscious; the ego confronts the images as though they were reality, not only perceiving them passively, but actively participating in their play and reaching an understanding with them. The images are self-manifestations of the psyche and may therefore be taken as fragments of those waking dreams dreamt below the threshold of consciousness, but which it does not perceive because of its preoccupation with processes in the external world. The aim of active imagination is to find a middle position between conscious and unconscious, having "a quality of conjoined opposites". ANIELA JAFFÉ, *The Myth Of Meaning In The Work Of C.G. Jung*

L. 129 "The unwary Soul that fails to grapple with the mocking demon of illusion, will return to earth the slave of Māra." HELENA PETROVNA BLAVATSKY, *The Voice of the Silence.*

L. 139 "To have lost the art of thinking in images is precisely to have lost the proper linguistic of metaphysics and to have descended to the verbal logic of philosophy." ANANDA COOMARASWAMY, *The Collected Works of Ananda Coomaraswamy.*

L. 142 "To the superficial observer, it will appear like madness. It would also have developed into one, had I not been able to absorb the overpowering force of the original experience. With the help of alchemy, I could finally arrange them into a whole" CARL JUNG, *Liber Novus*.

L. 152 "The highest and most intense activity of the mind consist of establishing models designed to stimulate another kind of mental activity about which it is little known and which moreover cannot be easily set in motion it is in this sense that we can say: everything is a symbol, everything is a sign, everything is an evocation of another reality." JOSEPH CAMPBELL, *The Hero with a Thousand Faces*.

L. 156 "In Endymion, I leaped headlong into the sea, and thereby have become better acquainted with the Soundings, the quicksands, and the rocks, than if I had stayed upon the green shore, and piped a silly pipe, and took tea and comfortable advice." JOHN KEATS, *Letters*.

L. 164 "But if you recognize your own involvement you yourself must enter into the process with your personal reactions, just as if you were one of the fantasy figures, or rather, as if the drama being enacted before your eyes were real." CARL JUNG, *Mysterium Coniunctionis*.

L. 167 "A numinous experience is no guarantee of inner peace, not in the long run anyway" "The experience of meaning — which is what, ultimately, life is about — is by no means equivalent to nonsuffering; yet the resilience of the self-aware and self-transforming consciousness can fortify us against the perils of the irrational and the rational, against the world within and the world without." ANIELA JAFFE, *The Myth of Meaning*.

END CHORUS

P. 60 "Atlas, that on his brazen shoulders rolls Yon heaven, the
ancient mansion of the gods, Was by a goddess sire to Maia;
she To supreme Jove bore me, and called me Hermes; Attendant
on the king, his high behests I execute. To Delphi am I come,
This land where Phoebus from his central throne Utters to
mortals his high strain, declaring The present and the future;"
EURIPIDES, *Ion.*

L. 1 CARL JUNG in *Mysterium Coniunctionis* analysed the historical
similarity between archetypes and symbolic images and his
conclusion was that they "often show such a striking
resemblance to mythological motifs that one cannot help
regarding the cause of the individual fantasies as identical
with those that determined the collective and mythological
images. In other words, there is no ground for the assumption
that human beings in other epochs produced fantasies for quite
different reasons, or that their fantasy images sprang from quite
different idées forces, from ours."

L. 8 "It is the business of mythology proper and of the fairy tale
to reveal specific dangers and techniques of the dark interior
way from tragedy to comedy." JOSEPH CAMPBELL, *The Hero
with a Thousand Faces.*

L. 9 "Beware of weakly giving way to trivial sympathies. Nothing
should shake the truly great spirit which is not sufficiently
mighty to destroy it." PERCY SHELLEY's *Journal of Friday,
October* 14, 1821.

L. 11 Plato argues in The Republic that the ideal state, one which
ensured the maximum possible happiness for all its citizens
could only be brought into being by a ruler possessed of absolute
knowledge that was obtained through philosophical study.

L. 13   "It is a well-known fact that the ancients already distinguished between two sorts of dreams, of which only one sort was considered divine." "The highest stage would be one in which the process of freedom spreads up to what is eternal of the soul itself, within which alone free communication takes place between what is eternally objective and what is eternally subjective of the soul. The potency that binds the Eternal to what lies below and to the world of senses would be transcended; the soul would be transported to the otherworldly realm, and as it were, entirely to the world of spirits." F.W.J. CON SCHELLING, *The Abyss of Freedom Ages of the World.*

L. 16   "A dream that is not understood remains a mere occurrence; understood it becomes a living experience." CARL JUNG, *The Practice of Psychotherapy.*

L. 17   "Until you make your unconscious conscious, it will direct you and you will call it fate." CARL JUNG, *Aion.*

P. 62   'Asmenos ek thanatoio' in Latin means "glad to have escaped death" which is an excerpt from HOMER's *Odyssey.*

KURT WARD has privately published a number
of poetry collections and an audio recording of
Jazz compositions for solo piano. Born in the
United States but now resides in the Netherlands.
As a Senior Design Director at Koninklijke
Philips N.V., he leads multi-disciplinary teams
to support strategic partnerships with public
and private organizations to transform global
healthcare systems.
WWW.KURTRWARD.COM

REBECCA YANOVSKAYA is a freelance
illustrator working in the fantasy, sci-fi and horror
genres. She frequently illustrates mythological
stories, natural forces, and aesthetically strong
characters. As one of a few primarily ballpoint pen
artists working in fantastic realism, her work is
easy to identify. A combination of epic scope and
moody atmosphere define her signature style, in
what can be described as the "Art of the Sublime".
WWW.REBECCAYANOVSKAYA.COM

HARRY HUYBERS is a graphic designer, living
and working in The Netherlands. He has been
applying his craft across typography and graphic
design for over 30 years.
WWW.HARRYHUYBERS.COM

ISBN 9789083219202

CPSIA information can be obtained
at www.ICGtesting.com
Printed in the USA
LVHW081454190123
737425LV00004B/766